SEP 2007

P9-DCU-705

EXPLORING CONTINENTS

ASIA

Anita Ganeri

Heinemann Library
Chicago, Illinois

3 1267 14012 1920

© 2007 Heinemann Library
a division of Reed Elsevier Inc.
Chicago, Illinois

Customer Service 888-454-2279
Visit our website at www.heinemannraintree.com

All rights reserved. No part of this publication may be reproduced or transmitted in any form or by any means, electronic or mechanical, including photocopying, recording, taping, or any information storage and retrieval system, without permission in writing from the publisher.

Designed by Richard Parker and Q2A Solutions
Illustrations by Jeff Edwards
Printed and bound in China by WKT

11 10 09 08 07
10 9 8 7 6 5 4 3 2 1

Library of Congress Cataloging-in-Publication Data
Ganeri, Anita, 1961-
  Asia / Anita Ganeri.-- 1st ed.
     p. cm. -- (Exploring continents)
  Includes bibliographical references and index.
  ISBN 1-4034-8243-8 (library binding-harcover) -- ISBN 1-4034-8251-9 (pbk.)
  1. Asia--Geography--Juvenile literature. I. Title. II. Series.
  DS5.92.G36 2006
  915--dc22
                              2006001159

Acknowledgments
The author and publishers are grateful to the following for permission to reproduce copyright material:
Alamy pp. **8** (Danita Delimont), **9** (Viewstock China), **10** (Alan Compton), **14** (Stefan Auth), **16** (Denis Fast), **25** (James Gritz); Corbis pp. **13** (Frans Lanting), **15** (Theo Allofs), **18** (Bojan Brecelj), **24** (Richard T. Nowitz), **27** (Jose Fuste Raga); Getty pp. **5** (Stone), **11** (National Geographic), **21** (Asia Images), **22** (Photonica), **23** (Stone); Superstock p. **19**; Travel Ink p. **7**.

Cover satellite image of Asia reproduced with permission of SPL/M-Sat Ltd.

Disclaimer
All the internet addresses (URLs) given in this book were valid at the time of going to press. However, due to the dynamic nature of the internet, some addresses may have changed or the sites may have ceased to exist since publication. While the author and publishers regret any inconvenience this may cause readers, no responsibility for such changes can be accepted by either the author(s) or the publishers.

Every effort has been made to contact copyright holders of any material reproduced in this book. Any omissions will be rectified in subsequent
printings if notice is given to the publishers.

CONTENTS

Words that appear in the text in bold, **like this**, are explained in the Glossary.

WHAT IS A CONTINENT?

About two-thirds of Earth is covered in water. The rest of Earth is made up of seven huge pieces of land called **continents**. Each of the continents, apart from Antarctica, is divided up into smaller regions called countries. This book is about the continent of Asia.

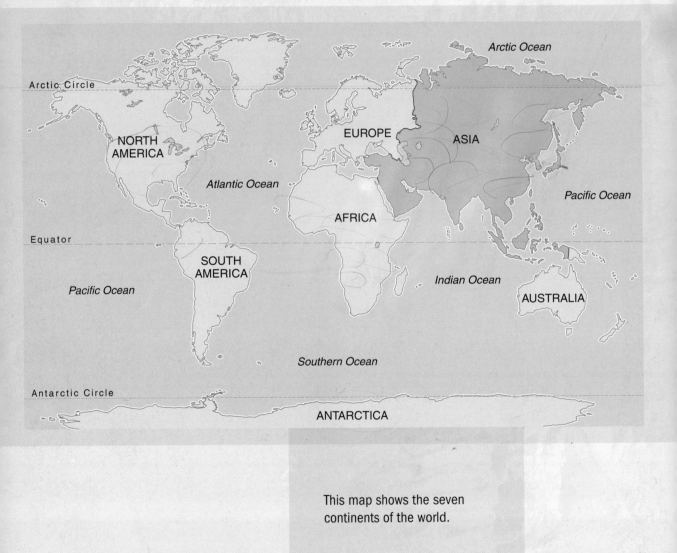

This map shows the seven continents of the world.

How big is Asia?

Asia is the world's largest continent. It covers almost one-third of Earth's land surface. It stretches from Africa and Europe in the west to the Pacific Ocean in the east. The northern part of Asia lies in the icy Arctic. Asia stretches southward to the hot, steamy places around the **equator**. Because of its enormous size, Asia has a wide range of **climates** and landscapes.

Islands and coasts

Thousands of islands form part of Asia. These islands include Sri Lanka, most of Indonesia, the Philippines, and Japan. Asia's coastline measures about 80,778 miles (130,000 kilometers). If it could be stretched out, it would be long enough to reach three times around the equator.

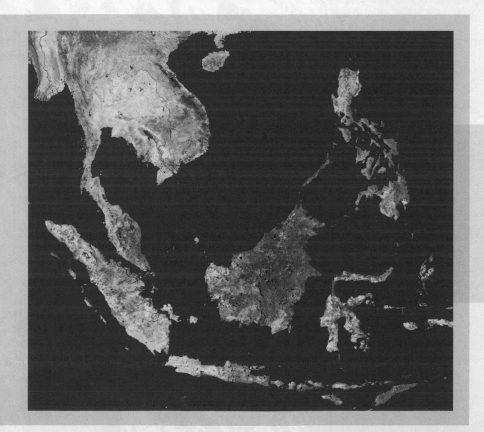

Indonesia is the world's largest **archipelago** (group of islands). It is made up of more than 13,600 islands, but people only live on about 6,000 of them.

WHAT DOES ASIA LOOK LIKE?

Asia is so enormous that it has almost every type of landscape. It has some of the world's driest deserts, longest rivers, largest lakes, and biggest forests. The highest (Mount Everest) and lowest (Dead Sea) points on Earth are both in Asia.

Record-breaking mountains

Many of the world's greatest mountains are found in the continent of Asia. In the west, the Ural Mountains in Russia divide Asia and Europe. The Pamir Mountains in Central Asia rise over 24,606 feet (7,500 meters).

This map shows some of the dramatic natural features found in Asia.

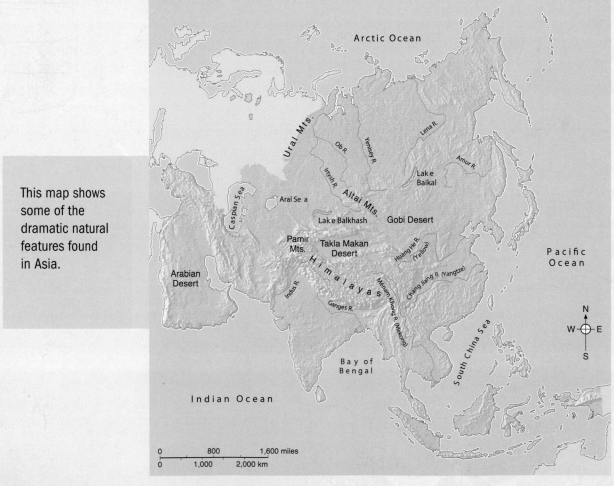

Hundreds of climbers have died in their attempts to reach the summit (top) of Mount Everest.

On top of the world

The most famous mountains in Asia are the Himalayas, which are to the north of India and Nepal. The Himalayas are the highest mountain range on Earth, with nine out of ten of the world's highest peaks.

At 29,035 feet (8,850 meters), Mount Everest in the Himalayas is the world's highest mountain. The first people to reach the top of Everest were the Nepalese climber Tenzing Norgay and the New Zealander Edmund Hillary, in May 1953.

The Gobi Desert stretches along the border between China and Mongolia.

Spreading deserts

Large parts of Western and Central Asia are covered by desert. The Arabian Desert in Saudi Arabia contains the Rub al Khali, or Empty Quarter, a huge sandy desert that covers an area of 250,965 square miles (650,000 square kilometers). The Kyzlkum Desert stretches across Kazakhstan and Uzebekistan. The Karakum covers most of Turkmenistan. The Thar Desert lies across the border of India and Pakistan. Farther east lies the Takla Makan Desert in China.

Large lakes

Asia has many large lakes. The largest lake in the world is the Caspian Sea. It covers 143,250 square miles (371,000 square kilometers) and lies partly in Azerbaijan, Iran, Turkmenistan, Kazakhstan, and Russia. This enormous lake is called a sea because it is filled with salt water.

Lake Baikal in Siberia is the deepest lake on Earth. It is up to 5,315 feet (1,620 meters) deep. It is famous for its wildlife, including the world's only freshwater seal.

Raging rivers

The Tigris and Euphrates rivers flow from Turkey across Iraq. The world's first **civilizations** grew up on the rich farmland between these two rivers. The Ganges River flows from the Himalayas across northern India to the Bay of Bengal, in India and Bangladesh. There, it joins the Brahmaputra River to form the world's largest river **delta**.

The Yangtze River in China is the longest river in Asia and the third longest river on Earth.

Did you know?

The Dead Sea in Israel and Jordan is the lowest place on Earth. It is 1,312 feet (400 meters) below sea level. Like the Caspian Sea, the Dead Sea is a saltwater lake. It got its name because its water is so salty that almost nothing can live in it.

WHAT IS THE WEATHER LIKE IN ASIA?

Asia is such a big place that is has a wide range of climates. In the far north, the weather is bitterly cold. On the deserts and plains in the center of the continent, almost no rain falls. These are some of the driest places on Earth. In the south of Asia, around the equator, the weather is hot and sticky all year round.

Monsoons

Winds called monsoons play an important part in Asia's weather. In summer, these winds bring very heavy rain to places like India and Sri Lanka. Farmers rely on this rain to water their fields. If there is not enough rain, their crops will be ruined. But if the rain is too heavy, it can flood their fields.

The monsoon rains can flood cities and force people to leave their homes.

Reindeer find very little to eat on the frozen Siberian **tundra**.

Frozen ground

Siberia is part of Russia. It lies in the far north of Asia. This huge region stretches from the Ural Mountains in the west across to the Pacific Ocean in the east. In the far north of Siberia, the climate is so cold that the top layers of the ground stay frozen all year round. Very few plants can survive here.

Wild weather

Each year, some parts of Asia are hit by tropical storms called **typhoons**. These storms bring winds traveling at over 125 miles (200 kilometers) per hour and can kill people and destroy buildings. The places most at risk are along the coast. These are low-lying, so they are easily flooded by the high waves whipped up by the winds.

ASIA'S WEATHER FACTS

◉ *Highest recorded temperature:* Tirat Tsvi, Israel: 129 °F (53.8 °C)

◉ *Lowest recorded temperature:* Oimekon and Verkhoyansk in Russia: minus 90 °F (minus 67.8 °C)

◉ *Highest average rainfall:* Mawsyrnram, India: 467.4 inches (11,872 mm) per year

◉ *Lowest average rainfall:* Aden, Yemen: 1.8 inches (46 mm) per year

WHAT PLANTS AND ANIMALS LIVE IN ASIA?

Asia has a wide range of **habitats**, from mountains to deserts to rain forests. These habitats provide homes to an amazing number of plants and animals.

Northern forest

The largest forest in the world stretches across Siberia. The trees in the forest are **coniferous**, which means that most of them do not lose their leaves in winter. They are well **adapted** to the cold Siberian weather. Their leaves are needle-shaped so that they do not lose too much water and dry out. Their branches bend easily so that heavy snow can slide off without snapping them.

This map shows the range of different kinds of plants that can be found in Asia.

Mangrove swamps

Farther south, muddy **mangrove** swamps grow along some coasts where rivers flow into the sea. There are large swamps around the Bay of Bengal in India and Bangladesh and in the Philippines, Thailand, and Indonesia. The swamps are filled with mangrove trees. These trees have two types of roots. Some roots fix the trees firmly in the mud to stop the tides from washing them away. Other roots stick out of the water. They take in air for the trees.

Near the equator, the climate is warm and sticky all year round. Tropical rain forests grow here. Valuable products, such as rubber, wood, spices, and medicines, come from rain forest plants.

The rafflesia is a plant that has the world's largest flower. It measures up to over 3 feet (1 meter) across. It grows in the rain forests of Borneo and Sumatra in Southeast Asia. Its enormous orange-brown flower smells of rotting meat!

Camels are perfectly adapted for living in the desert. They can store fat in their bodies for food.

Life in the desert

It is difficult for animals to live in Asia's deserts because the deserts are so hot and dry. Even so, many animals have adapted to desert life. Camels can go for days without drinking water. They have big, flat feet for walking over sand and can close their nostrils to keep sand out.

Many small desert animals spend the day underground in their burrows, taking shelter from the heat. They come out at night when it is cooler. Jerboas are small, furry animals that live in the deserts of Asia. They always walk upright and can hop faster than a person can run.

Mountain animals

Mountains, such as the Himalayas, have many different places for animals to live. Bears live in the forests that cover the bottom of the mountain slopes. Higher up, where it is colder and windier, animals such as yaks, snow leopards, and antelopes live. Vultures fly above the mountain slopes, looking for dead animals to eat.

Animals in danger

Many of the animals that live in Asia's forests are in danger of dying out because their wild homes are being destroyed. Giant pandas live in the mountain forests of Southwest China. They feed mainly on **bamboo**. As the forests are cut down to make farmland, the pandas are losing their supply of food.

The Komodo dragon's tongue picks up scents to help it find food.

Did you know?

The Komodo dragon is the world's largest lizard. It can grow to be almost 10 feet (3 meters) long. It lives only on Komodo and a few other islands in Indonesia. The dragon eats wild pigs, deer, and goats, which it swallows whole.

15

Arctic animals

Animals that live in freezing Siberia have to be tough to survive. But they have special features to help them. The snowy owl has thick feathers to keep it warm. Its feathers have black and white speckles. The color and pattern help to hide the owl against the snow as it hunts for voles and other small animals to eat.

The snowy owl has to have extremely good eyesight to hunt in this difficult terrain.

WHAT ARE ASIA'S NATURAL RESOURCES?

Asia has many **natural resources**. Some countries, such as Saudi Arabia, Japan, and China, have used their natural resources to build up strong industries. This has helped them to become rich. But many countries, such as Bangladesh and Nepal, have not developed so quickly. They are still very poor. People in these countries mainly work as farmers.

Useful resources

The Middle East in Southwest Asia produces a lot of the world's oil. Before oil was discovered, the countries in the Middle East were quite poor. But selling oil has made them very rich. Oil and gas also comes from the tiny country of Brunei in Southeast Asia. Malaysia produces large amounts of **palm oil** and rubber. Myanmar and Sri Lanka are famous for their gemstones, including sapphires and rubies.

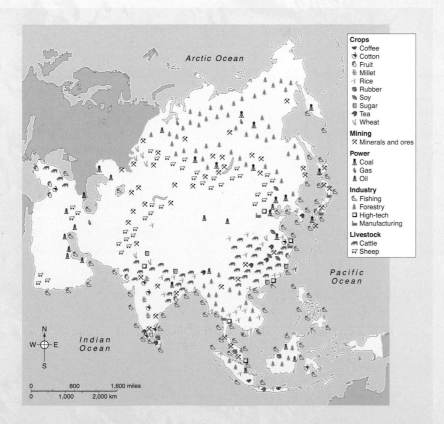

This map shows where different natural resources can be found in Asia.

Taiwan is well known for producing many different kinds of electronic goods.

Growing industries

Many Asian countries have important industries. China, India, Japan, Russia, Taiwan, and South Korea have many modern factories. These factories make cars, iron, steel, weapons, ships, and machinery. Japan is one of the top industrial countries in the world. Japanese businesses **export** huge amounts of goods, from cars to computers. Countries such as China and India are working hard to build up their industries.

Tourism

Tourism makes a lot of money for many Asian countries. Thousands of tourists from all over the world visit countries such as Thailand, Indonesia, and Sri Lanka. They go to see the breathtaking scenery and beautiful buildings and to relax on the golden, sandy beaches.

Farming

Over half of all the people in Asia earn their living by farming. In many Asian countries, farmers do not use modern farm machinery. Their farms are often very small. The farmers struggle to grow enough crops to feed their families and to sell at market. Some Asian countries, such as Japan and Israel, have large, modern farms. They use modern **irrigation** systems to grow large amounts of crops.

Major crops

The most important crops grown in Asia are rice and wheat. Rice is the main food for many Asian people. Most of the world's tea and rubber also comes from Asia. Other crops include cotton, **jute**, and sugarcane.

Many Asian farmers still use hand tools and animals, such as water buffalo, to pull their **plows**.

WHAT COUNTRIES AND CITIES ARE IN ASIA?

Asia is divided into 50 countries. Most of these are whole countries, but part of Turkey and part of Russia also lie in Asia. The rest of Turkey and Russia are in Europe. China is the largest country that lies wholly in Asia. It covers 3,705,422 square miles (9,597,000 square kilometers). The smallest country is the tiny island country of the Maldives. It covers just 115 square miles (300 square kilometers).

This map shows all the countries in Asia. It is easy to see how much they vary in size.

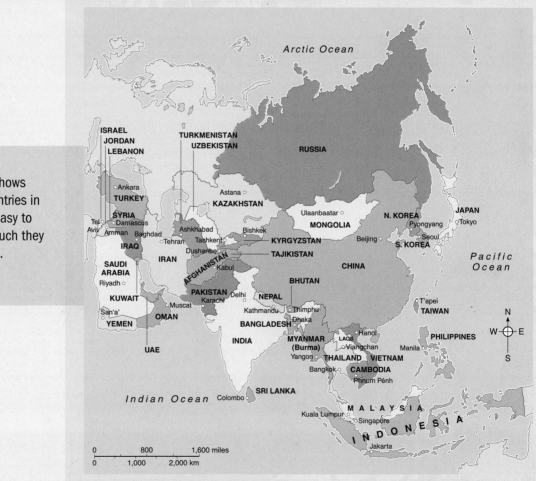

Asian history

Asia has a long history. The world's first civilizations grew up in Asia about 5,500 years ago. They built the world's first cities and farms. People from Asia also invented the first system of writing.

From the 1500s, Europeans came to Asia to trade. They wanted to take the wealth of Asian countries for themselves. European countries, such as Great Britain, Spain, and France, began to rule countries such as India, the Philippines, and Vietnam. During the 1900s, Asian countries gained their freedom from these foreign rulers.

Government and politics

Today, the countries of Asia are governed in many different ways. Bhutan, Saudi Arabia, and Thailand are ruled by kings. Brunei is ruled by a **sultan**. Bahrain and Qatar have leaders called **sheiks**. **Communist governments** rule China, North Korea, and Vietnam. Countries including India, Israel, Mongolia, Japan, and South Korea are **democracies**.

This photograph shows the sultan of Brunei on the grounds of his palace.

Cities of Asia

Asia's cities are growing very fast. This is because many poor people are moving from the country into the cities to search for work. Many cities now have more than ten million people living in them. The largest cities on the continent are Mumbai in India (thirteen million people), Seoul in South Korea (twelve million people), and Karachi in Pakistan (eleven million people).

Did you know?

Istanbul in Turkey (above) is the only city in the world that is split between two continents. Part of it lies in Asia and part in Europe. The two parts of the city are separated by a narrow stretch of water called the Bosphorus. Istanbul is the largest city in Turkey.

WHO LIVES IN ASIA?

Today, almost 4,000 million people live in Asia. This means about three out of every five people on Earth live in Asia. Asia has seven out of ten of the world's most crowded countries. China and India are at the top of the list. Between them, these two countries are home to about 40 percent of the world's population.

Population figures

Some parts of Asia are very crowded, particularly along the coasts, river valleys, and in the big cities. This is where it is easier for people to grow crops or find jobs. Very few people live in places such as the deserts or the frozen north.

Some cities, like Tokyo in Japan, have become very big and busy. People come to live there to find jobs.

The Bedouin wander through the desert in search of food and water for their animals.

The people of Asia

The people of Asia follow many different ways of life, speak different languages, and have different religious beliefs. In Southwest Asia, Arabs are the largest group of people. They speak Arabic and follow the religion of Islam. Some Arabs, called Bedouin, live as **nomads**. The Bedouin live in tents that are light and easy to carry.

In East Asia, Chinese people make up most of the population. Many Chinese people have also settled in other Asian countries, such as Malaysia and Singapore.

Asian languages

Thousands of different languages are spoken in Asia. Many people speak more than one language. Mandarin Chinese is spoken by more people than any other language. More than one billion people speak it. Other widely spoken Asian languages are Hindustani, Arabic, Bengali, and Japanese.

Religions of Asia

All six of the world's main religions began in Asia. They are Buddhism, Christianity, Hinduism, Islam, Judaism, and Sikhism. Religion is still very important in the lives of the people of Asia.

- Hinduism is the main faith in India and Nepal.
- Many people in Southwest and Central Asia are Muslims who follow Islam.
- Buddhism is followed in Southeast Asia and is also widespread in Sri Lanka, Tibet, China, and Japan.
- Judaism is the main religion in Israel.
- Sikhism started in the Punjab, now divided between Pakistan and India.
- Christianity is widespread in the Philippines and parts of Russia.

Buddhist monks across Asia pray to statues of the Buddha. These monks are in Cambodia.

25

WHAT FAMOUS PLACES ARE IN ASIA?

Asia has an amazing number of famous places. They range from natural wonders to ancient ruins and modern landmarks.

Natural wonders

Asia has many natural wonders. Mount Fuji in Japan is one of the most famous mountains in Asia. It is 12,388 feet (3,776 meters) high. Its perfect cone shape can be seen from miles around. Mount Fuji has become a symbol of Japan.

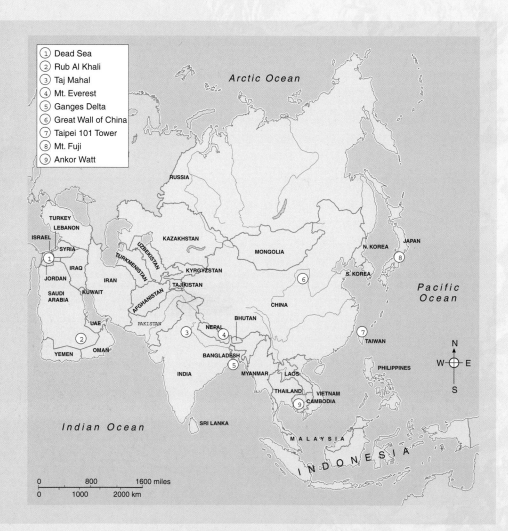

1. Dead Sea
2. Rub Al Khali
3. Taj Mahal
4. Mt. Everest
5. Ganges Delta
6. Great Wall of China
7. Taipei 101 Tower
8. Mt. Fuji
9. Ankor Watt

This map shows some of the amazing wonders found in Asia.

Ancient landmarks

Many ancient buildings are found in Asia. The Great Wall of China stretches for over 4,500 miles (7,300 kilometers) across northern China. Built over thousands of years, it was meant to keep invaders out of the country. It is the only human-made structure that can be seen from space!

The Taj Mahal was built in India in the 1600s by Emperor Shah Jahan. It was a memorial for his dead wife. It is built from white marble and took over twenty years to finish. The inside of the building is decorated with precious and semi-precious stones.

Modern landmarks

Asia has many modern landmarks and buildings. One of the most striking is the luxurious Burj al Arab Hotel in Dubai, in the United Arab Emirates. The TFC 101 Tower in Taipei, Taiwan, was built in 2004. It is 1,666 feet (508 meters) high. Super-fast elevators carry passengers to the top of the 91-story tower in just 30 seconds.

The Burj al Arab Hotel overlooks the sea and is shaped like an enormous ship's sail. It was built in 1999.

27

CONTINENTS COMPARISON CHART

Continent	Area	Population	
AFRICA	11,720,000 square miles (30,365,000 square kilometers)	approximately 906 million	
ANTARCTICA	5,500,000 square miles (14,200,000 square kilometers)	Officially none, but about 4,000 people live in the research stations during the summer and over 3,000 people visit as tourists each year. People have lived there for as long as three and a half years at a time.	
ASIA	17,226,200 square miles (44,614,000 square kilometers)	approximately 4,000 million	
AUSTRALIA	2,966,136 square miles (7,713,364 square kilometers)	approximately 20,090,400 (2005 estimate)	
EUROPE	4,000,000 square miles (10,400,000 square kilometers)	approximately 727 million (2005 estimate)	
NORTH AMERICA	9,355,000 square miles (24,230,000 square kilometers)	approximately 509,915,000 (2005 estimate)	
SOUTH AMERICA	6,878,000 square miles (17,814,000 square kilometers)	approximately 380 million	

Number of Countries	Highest Point	Longest River
54 (includes Western Sahara)	Mount Kilimanjaro, Tanzania: 19,340 feet (5,895 meters)	Nile River: 4,160 miles (6,695 kilometers)
none, but over 23 countries have research stations in Antarctica	Vinson Massif: 16,067 feet (4,897 meters)	Onyx River: 7.5 miles (12 kilometers) **Biggest Ice Shelf** Ross Ice Shelf in western Antarctica: 600 miles (965 kilometers) long
50	Mount Everest, Tibet and Nepal: 29,035 feet (8,850 meters)	Yangtze River, China: 3,914 miles (6,300 kilometers)
1	Mount Kosciusko: 7,313 feet (2,229 meters)	Murray River: 1,566 miles (2,520 kilometers)
47	Mount Elbrus, Russia: 18,510 feet (5,642 meters)	Volga River: 2,290 miles (3,685 kilometers)
23	Mount McKinley (Denali) in Alaska: 20,320 feet (6,194 meters)	Mississippi/Missouri River system: 3,895 miles (6,270 kilometers)
12	Aconcagua, Argentina: 22,834 feet (6,959 meters)	Amazon River: 4,000 miles (6,400 kilometers)

GLOSSARY

adapted when plants or animals have special features to help them live in a place

archipelago group of islands

bamboo tall tropical plant with grassy leaves and thin wooden stems

civilization ancient people and their culture

climate weather places usually have over a long time

communist government government that owns all its country's land and controls all its people's jobs

coniferous trees that have needles instead of leaves and grow cones. Most conifers do not lose their leaves in winter.

continent one of Earth's largest landmasses

delta land formed from sand and mud where a river flows into the sea

democracy country ruled by a government that has been elected by the people

equator imaginary line around the middle of Earth

export to sell to other countries

habitat place where plants and animals live

irrigation how water is brought to farmers' fields

jute plant fibers used to make mats, sacks, and ropes

mangrove plants that grows in coastal swamps

natural resources country's stocks of coal, oil, metals, and so on

nomad person who moves from place to place

palm oil oil from palm trees that is used in many products, including bread, chocolate, potato chips, and cleaning products

plow piece of farm machinery used for digging up the soil

sheikh chief or leader in the Arab world

sultan title of a Muslim king

tundra flat land where there are few trees and the soil is partly frozen all year

typhoon tropical storm; also known as a hurricane or cyclone

Books

Green, Jen. *Destination Detectives: Japan*. Chicago: Raintree, 2006.

McClish, Bruce. *Old World Continents: Africa, Europe, & Asia*. Chicago: Heinemann Library, 2004.

Spilsbury, Richard. *Rivers Through Time: Settlements of the Ganges River*. Chicago: Heinemann Library, 2005.

Townsend, Sue, and Caroline Young. *A World of Recipes: Indonesia*. Chicago: Heinemann Library, 2003.

Useful websites

- Lots of facts, figures, statistics, and maps about the world's continents, countries, cities, languages, and people:
http://www.worldatlas.com

- Profiles of Asian countries, details of current events, and information about every aspect of Asian art, religion, culture, and politics:
http://www.askasia.org

- Map-based games based on the countries and capital cities of Asia:
http://www.sheppardsoftware.com/Asian_Geography